Blockchain for everyone

Stefano Della Valle

December 2024

Index

1. Introduction

Blockchain is a technology that, in just over a decade, has captured the imagination of innovators, technologists, and entrepreneurs worldwide. Often associated with cryptocurrencies like Bitcoin and Ethereum, blockchain is far more than a mere infrastructure for value transfer. It is a decentralized and secure system that enables the transparent and immutable management of information and transactions, paving the way for new possibilities across a wide range of applications.

Its functionality is built on key concepts such as the distributed ledger, consensus mechanisms, and smart contracts, which together provide a robust platform for creating secure and reliable digital ecosystems. However, blockchain is not just a technology; it is also a cultural and organizational revolution. It challenges traditional centralized models, introducing a paradigm rooted in transparency, decentralization, and mathematical trust, rather than reliance on centralized authorities.

From understanding the blockchain trilemma—balancing security, scalability, and decentralization—to exploring practical applications such as decentralized finance (DeFi), NFTs, supply chain traceability, and digital identity, the journey into blockchain reveals how this technology is transforming entire economic and social sectors.

Despite its immense promise, blockchain is a complex technology that is often misunderstood and, at times, overhyped. Its potential must be tempered with a critical understanding of its limitations, costs, and risks. In these pages, we will delve into not only the foundational principles but also the technical and practical details that make blockchain one of the most disruptive and, simultaneously, most debated technologies of our time.

The future of blockchain is unwritten. It is up to us to understand, adapt, and shape it to meet the challenges of an increasingly digital, global, and interconnected world.

2. Basic Concepts

2.1. Centralized, Distributed, and Decentralized

To fully understand the concepts of distribution and decentralization, often confused or misused, we need to take a step back in history to 1964, when Prof. Paul Baran of the RAND Corporation was tasked with addressing one of the greatest national security challenges: protecting the United States' telecommunications infrastructure from a potential nuclear attack during the Cold War.

At the time, telecommunications networks were primarily centralized, structured around a main node that managed and routed communications to subordinate nodes. This model had a critical vulnerability: if the central node were destroyed, the entire network would collapse, rendering communication impossible.

Baran proposed two alternatives: a decentralized network and a distributed network. These are two distinct models that are often confused, yet they have fundamental differences.

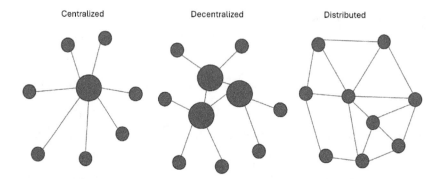

Centralized · Decentralized · Distributed

In a decentralized network, control and the flow of information are delegated to multiple main nodes. Each central node is responsible for a subgroup of smaller nodes, forming a hierarchical, multi-level structure. This approach improves resilience compared to a centralized network: if a main node is compromised, the subordinate nodes can continue to function by connecting to other main nodes. However, the network is not fully autonomous, as the loss of multiple central nodes can still compromise its overall integrity.

A distributed network represents a more advanced concept, where no central node exists. All nodes are equal and communicate directly with one another, forming a structure in which every node acts as both sender and receiver of information. This model completely eliminates the risk of a single point of failure: even if some nodes are destroyed or disconnected, the remaining ones can continue to operate without interruption. The resilience of the network increases exponentially as the number of nodes grows.

A practical example of a decentralized network is the traditional postal system. Each central post office serves a specific geographic area, and if one office ceases to function, part of its operations can be redirected to other central offices, ensuring at least a minimum level of service.

A practical example of a distributed network is the peer-to-peer (P2P) system, as seen in early file-sharing platforms like Napster or BitTorrent. Each participant in the network acts as both a provider and a consumer of resources, ensuring that the system continues to operate even when significant numbers of nodes are lost.

The practical application of these concepts emerged with the development of **ARPANET**, a project launched in the 1960s by the Advanced Research Projects Agency (ARPA) of the U.S. Department of Defense. ARPANET was conceived as a decentralized network in which several central nodes connected universities and research laboratories to share computational resources and information.

Over time, ARPANET evolved into the Internet, which combines elements of both decentralized and distributed networks. The Internet lacks a single control point or central node and is instead built on a global infrastructure of autonomous nodes that use standard protocols (like TCP/IP) to communicate. Each node can operate independently while collaborating to ensure global connectivity. This distributed approach is one of the reasons the Internet is considered highly resilient. Even in the event of large-scale failures, traffic can be rerouted through alternative nodes, maintaining the functionality of the network.

2.2. Organizational Decentralization

Although decentralization originated as an architectural model for communication networks, its principles are applicable to many aspects of human activity, offering significant advantages in terms of efficiency and resilience. A prime example is general elections, which adopt a decentralized vote-counting system. In this context, each polling station functions as an autonomous node that collects, verifies, and counts a limited number of ballots. This distribution of responsibilities enhances operational efficiency by spreading the workload across multiple actors, while simultaneously strengthening the security of the electoral process.

A decentralized system is inherently more robust against manipulation or attacks. To alter election results, the security of most polling stations would need to be compromised, a feat that is logistically and economically prohibitive. Conversely, in a centralized system, a single control point represents a critical vulnerability. If the central hub overseeing the process were attacked or suffered a malfunction, the entire system could be easily compromised or rendered unusable.

This comparison highlights how decentralization not only increases the resilience of a system but also reduces reliance on single points of failure. The robustness of decentralized systems, which rely on distributing labor and risk, makes them particularly suited to contexts where security, reliability, and fairness are paramount.

For some, the principle of decentralization should be more widely applied in organizations and systems that have a direct and significant impact on citizens' lives. A clear example of this need is the process that governs the value of money in a country, a crucial factor that influences the entire economy and, consequently, the quality of life.

Traditionally, the value of money is regulated by centralized entities such as central banks, which control the issuance of currency, monetary policies, and national reserves. While this model has ensured stability in many contexts, it is also vulnerable to human error, political pressure, or arbitrary decisions, all of which can have wide-ranging negative consequences. Hyperinflation, sudden currency devaluation, and crises of confidence in monetary management are just a few examples of what can happen when the centralized system governing money loses the trust of citizens.

Decentralization offers an alternative model that could mitigate some of these vulnerabilities. By adopting a distributed approach, key decisions about the value of money could be managed more transparently and resiliently. For example, blockchain-based cryptocurrencies like Bitcoin use a decentralized mechanism to govern the issuance and control of token value. There is no central authority regulating the network; instead, management is entrusted to a predefined protocol that is verifiable by all participants.

This transparency and resistance to manipulation make the decentralized model particularly appealing, especially in contexts where trust in central institutions is low. However, this approach is not without challenges. A decentralized system for managing money would require a very high level of participation and consensus among stakeholders, as well as advanced technology to ensure security and scalability. Moreover, the absence of a central authority could make it more difficult to respond quickly to sudden economic crises.

The debate between centralization and decentralization in monetary management reflects a broader tension between efficiency and resilience, centralized control, and distributed power. While traditional systems offer a consolidated structure, decentralized systems promise greater transparency and a reduction in vulnerabilities associated with the concentration of power.

2.3. The hash function

One of the fundamental characteristics of blockchain technology is its intrinsic security, which stems from the use of advanced cryptographic functions. Among these, the hash function stands out as one of the most iconic and critical components for ensuring data integrity.

To better understand its functionality, it can be compared to a mathematical function that calculates the average of a series of numbers. In this analogy, regardless of the length of the series, the result is always a single number, bounded by the minimum and maximum values of the series. Similarly, a hash function processes data of any size and outputs a fixed-length sequence of characters, known as a digest or simply a hash.

The key difference between an averaging function and a hash function lies in how the output responds to changes in the input. When adding a new number to the input of an averaging function, the output will change only slightly, unless the new value is significantly different from the rest. In contrast, even the smallest alteration to the input of a hash function— whether adding, removing, or modifying a single bit—results in a completely different output.

Moreover, the probability of two different inputs producing the same hash (a collision) is infinitesimally small, and it is computationally infeasible to deduce the original input data from its hash. These properties make hash functions indispensable for cryptographic applications.

One of the most common applications of hash functions is in **digital signatures**, where they play a pivotal role in verifying the authenticity and integrity of digital documents. By generating a unique hash for each document, any alteration to the content can be instantly detected, ensuring the security of transactions and communications in a digital ecosystem.

2.4. The Two-Factor Digital Signature

The signature of a document is a fundamental element in communication and human transactions. Whether the document is informational or contractual in nature, the signature ensures its authenticity and binding nature, preventing the signer from denying their responsibility. In the digital context, replicating this function requires advanced cryptographic technologies, primarily based on two components: the hash function and asymmetric encryption.

Asymmetric encryption relies on a pair of cryptographic keys, one private and one public, which are generated together and mathematically linked. The private key is used to encrypt data, while the associated public key enables its decryption. This relationship ensures that only the holder of the private key can generate a signature, and anyone with the corresponding public key can verify it.

In the digital signature process, the first step is calculating the hash of the document. This hash acts as a unique fingerprint, condensing the document's content into a fixed-length sequence. The hash is then encrypted with the signer's private key, producing the digital signature. The document, along with the digital signature and the public key, forms the signed document. Verification involves recalculating the hash of the received document and comparing it with the one decrypted from the digital signature using the public key. If the two hashes match, the document is confirmed as authentic and unaltered.

For a digital signature to have legal validity, the public key must be verifiably linked to the identity of the signer. This linkage is ensured by a digital certificate issued by a Certification Authority (CA), a trusted entity that verifies the identity of the private key holder and certifies its association with the public key. This certificate is an essential component for establishing trust and ensuring the reliability of digital signatures in legal and transactional contexts.

3. From the e-commerce to Bitcoin

When the internet emerged around 1990, it quickly became clear that this new technology would transform the way business was conducted. One of the most revolutionary changes was the ability to create online stores, allowing businesses to expand their markets globally. However, a fundamental problem arose: how could payments be made and received securely?

While remote commerce had already been a well-established practice in many countries for decades—consider the success of initiatives like Postalmarket in Italy or catalog sales in the United States—the advent of online commerce introduced new challenges. Traditional catalogs relied on trust fostered by the reputation of brands and established postal payment mechanisms, but this credibility did not easily translate to the early e-commerce sites.

At that time, trust in online stores was tenuous. Consumers often encountered websites with unclear product descriptions, sometimes available only in the seller's language, making it difficult for an international audience to assess the quality or even the nature of the product. This lack of transparency bred scepticisms, which hindered the adoption of online shopping.

On the other hand, online merchants faced a practical and seemingly insurmountable issue: how to ensure payment from customers. The options available were far from ideal. Merchants could not simply send goods in the hope that customers would later remember to make a bank transfer. The absence of a reliable intermediary for logistics and payments rendered the process too risky for both sellers and buyers. It became evident that a secure, fast, and universally accessible digital payment system was desperately needed.

Jeff Bezos, the founder of Amazon, recounts a telling anecdote. When Amazon first launched, selling only books at the time, orders were received via traditional mail. Some customers even included cash in the envelope to pay for their orders. This method was not only inconvenient and risky but also entirely unsustainable at scale. As e-commerce grew, the need for more efficient and secure payment systems became unavoidable.

In the years that followed, innovative solutions began to emerge. Services like PayPal allowed users to make online payments easily and securely using credit cards. This was revolutionary: for the first time, people could buy and sell online without the complications of traditional methods such as checks or cash. However, while most innovators focused on solutions built on traditional banking systems, a group of visionaries was working on something entirely different.

These pioneers were mathematicians and cryptography enthusiasts deeply concerned with privacy and the centralization of monetary systems. Their goal was not simply to improve online payments but to reinvent them from the ground up. They envisioned a digital currency that existed solely on the internet and could be used without the need for banks or credit cards—essentially eliminating intermediaries.

After years of attempts and failures, **Bitcoin** emerged in 2009, marking the birth of the first true cryptocurrency and the introduction of blockchain technology. Bitcoin was not just a payment system; it incorporated the core functions of a bank, such as transaction recording and verification, but without a central institution.

Before Bitcoin, many other digital currencies had been proposed, but they all shared the same critical issue: the risk of "double spending" (spending the same money twice). In the physical world, this problem is addressed by intermediaries—banks and financial institutions—that record every movement of money in a centralized system. Each payment is verified, recorded, and linked to a unique identifier to ensure that funds are properly transferred from the sender's account to the recipients.

Replicating this level of control in a digital environment without intermediaries proved challenging. Early attempts at digital currencies had users managing their accounts independently, like small private banks. This approach was vulnerable, as it was easy to alter ledger to generate money. Furthermore, the role of a central bank to issue and regulate the currency was undefined.

Bitcoin's breakthrough innovation was the introduction of a ledger that records all transactions made by all users—essentially the instructions for transferring units of value from one account to another. In practice, blockchain functions as a single, large accounting book shared among all users.

Unlike traditional banking systems, where each institution records only its clients' transactions and coordinates with a central bank to ensure consistency across the various ledgers, blockchain allows every user to maintain a complete copy of the ledger. This eliminates the need for a central authority and ensures the security of transactions.

Thanks to this innovation, Bitcoin created an entirely new financial system, one that is decentralized and built on mathematical trust rather than human intermediaries. It was the first step toward a future where transactions no longer require banks but instead rely on a network of people and computers working together to verify and secure every operation.

Since Bitcoin's creation—the first and still the most significant blockchain—many other projects have emerged. However, all blockchains share the same fundamental component: a shared ledger where all transactions are recorded.

4. The distributed ledger

The question naturally arises: where is a blockchain ledger stored? The answer to this question helps us understand one of the most important aspects of blockchains: the ledger is not stored in a specific location but on numerous computers distributed all over the world. This is the core of blockchain technology and what gives its name to this technological field: **Distributed Ledger Technology (DLT).**

In practice, the ledger is hosted on many computers that communicate with each other to create a network.

The term "blockchain" does not merely refer to a chain of blocks containing transactions but more broadly represents the entire set of procedures, software, and protocols upon which the network's operation depends. This includes copies of the ledger and the users, who, through their wallets, effectively constitute a functional element of the network itself.

In general, a user can connect to any network node and access a copy of the ledger. Each node is interchangeable and equivalent. However, one cannot blindly trust any particular node; for this reason, high-profile users often activate their own node.

In blockchain technology, the network is composed of **trustless** and **permissionless** nodes, with the guiding principle being "trust no one."

- **Trustless** means that regardless of who operates a node—often it's not even possible to know this—a user should not assume that the node is reliable or that it holds a correct copy of the ledger. This explains why it is advisable to have one's own node or use multiple nodes simultaneously to cross-check the information obtained.

- **Permissionless** means that anyone can activate a node. This ensures that no user is dependent on someone else's node, which could, to some extent, act as an intermediary, partially compromising the logic of decentralization that underpins blockchain technology.

4.1. Private blockchains

To provide a complete picture, it is important to highlight that there are blockchains composed of **permissioned nodes**, which are networks where a node or a group of nodes oversees and controls who can access the ledger for reading and who has permission to create transactions. This model introduces an element of centralization, as the supervising authority acts as a central entity managing access and operations within the network.

These blockchains are commonly referred to as **private blockchains** or **consortium blockchains**, depending on whether control is exercised by a single entity or a small group of actors.

Despite some technical similarities with public blockchains, such as the block structure and the use of cryptography for security, private and centralized blockchains differ substantially in their architecture and fundamental principles. The presence of a supervising entity undermines the element of decentralization—one of the cornerstones of blockchain technology—and makes these networks more akin to traditional centralized systems.

As a result, they cannot fully benefit from the security, transparency, and reliability typical of public blockchains, which we will discuss from this point forward.

5. Distributed ledger security

Is having many copies of a registry really safer than having one copy on a robust cloud operated by operators such as Amazon, Google, or Microsoft?

Certainly, compared to traditional storage methods, the distributed ledger presents greater complexity and difficulty of use. However, this complexity brings with it huge benefits in terms of security, resilience and transparency.

So, the answer is yes.

5.1. Failure resistance

In traditional systems, such as centralized storage, data is stored in a single container, such as a physical server or database. This model has an inherent vulnerability: if that container suffers damage, such as a hardware failure, cyberattack, or human error, data can be irretrievably lost. To mitigate these risks, more complex storage models, such as cloud computing, have been developed, which distribute data across multiple servers and locations, often located in different countries or continents.

The cloud, as its name suggests, is designed to eliminate a precise relationship between digital content and a storage or processing device. However, this infrastructure is not immune to failures. Due to the enormous complexity of cloud computing platforms and the multiple interconnections between the systems that compose them, even the most famous service providers have faced disastrous accidents that have caused massive damage to their users.

A significant example is the case of **AWS (Amazon Web Services)** in 2017, when human error during routine maintenance led to the temporary shutdown of a significant portion of the network in the United States, causing disruptions to critical services for many businesses and platforms, such as Trello and Quora. Similarly, **Google Cloud** suffered a network failure in 2019 that heavily impacted global services such as Gmail, YouTube and Shopify, disrupting the operations of millions of users for several hours.

Microsoft Azure, one of the leading global cloud platforms, has also experienced similar events. In 2021, a series of power blackouts at a data center in Texas caused data inaccessibility for many companies, highlighting how unpredictable external factors can still affect systems designed to be highly resilient.

These episodes show that despite huge technological advances, centralized or semi-centralized systems, such as cloud computing, remain vulnerable to large-scale failure.

Conversely, since every node in the network that supports the distributed ledger maintains a complete copy of the ledger, even if many nodes were to stop, a blockchain would continue to function without any side effects. To this must be added that the probability that half of the nodes, distributed all over the world, go offline at the same time, is absolutely negligible.

5.2. Resistance to cyber attacks

Cloud-based systems, and even more so those based on centralized physical servers, have an inherent vulnerability: the fact that they centralize data and processes in specific points makes them relatively easy targets for cyberattacks. Hackers, aware of the importance and concentration of resources in these infrastructures, are constantly developing new techniques to overcome defenses, making security a constant game of chase between attackers and sysops, i.e. the technicians responsible for managing and protecting systems.

Large cloud computing platforms, such as those offered by Amazon Web Services (AWS), Microsoft Azure or Google Cloud, invest billions of dollars in infrastructure and security to protect customer data, but the concentration of resources in centralized data centers is still attractive to cybercriminals. Incidents such as the 2017 **Cloud Hopper Attack**, which saw nation-state-sponsored hacking groups breach numerous cloud service providers, show that even industry giants are not immune to these threats.

Another concrete example is the attack suffered by **Equifax** in 2017. Although the company did not use a purely cloud infrastructure, the centralized system for managing the sensitive data of millions of people was breached, with the theft of personal information of more than 140 million individuals. This attack, one of the most devastating in history, highlighted how centralizing data in a single point constitutes a critical vulnerability.

There are many countermeasures to mitigate these risks. They range from the implementation of advanced firewalls and intrusion detection systems to the encryption of data both in transit and at rest, to the segmentation of networks to isolate potential entry points. However, each new security measure comes with significant costs, both in terms of implementation and maintenance. For example, AI-powered security systems to detect anomalous activity require expensive infrastructure and continuous updating to remain effective.

This dynamic between hackers and sysops represents an endless competition. Hackers are developing increasingly sophisticated techniques, such as ransomware-based attacks, which encrypt entire systems until a ransom is paid, or distributed denial of service (DDoS) attacks, which overload servers and render them unusable. Instead, sysops must implement increasingly advanced defensive measures, such as adopting blockchain-based protection technologies to ensure data integrity or distributing workloads across global infrastructures to mitigate the effects of attacks.

This competition inevitably results in increased operating costs. Service providers must continually update their technologies, train staff to deal with new threats, and invest in security audits and certifications to reassure customers. For example, according to recent studies, companies spend an average **of 15-20% of their IT budget** on security alone, a percentage that continues to grow.

As threats become increasingly sophisticated, traditional systems based on centralized servers or centralized cloud infrastructures face a growing challenge: ensuring security without compromising economic and operational efficiency. This is one of the reasons why decentralized architectures, such as blockchain-based ones, are emerging as attractive alternatives in industries where security is crucial.

Attacking a distributed ledger, on the other hand, requires simultaneously hitting all nodes that replicate the ledger. As the number of nodes in the network increases, the complexity of an attack grows exponentially. A sufficiently large network makes a cyber-attack practically impossible, both for practical limitations and for unsustainable costs. This ensures a level of security that does not depend on the strict protection of a single node, but on the robustness of the entire system.

Thanks to this structure, there is no need to take expensive defense measures to protect each node from sophisticated cyberattacks. The cost of running a node remains extremely low and will be forever, regardless of network growth. Added to this is another distinctive feature: the blockchain is open and replicable. Anyone can get a copy of the registry by simply activating a node. Trying to hack a node to access its data is therefore futile, since the same data is publicly available.

This approach fundamentally changes the paradigm of data security in critical applications. In traditional banking systems, for example, a bank account number is not considered a critical piece of data, as transaction and balance details remain confidential. In a distributed ledger, however, the exact opposite happens: all transactions are public and visible, but the identity of the account owners (address) is protected. Each address is generated from a private key, known only to the owner. If the owner does not disclose their address, even if hackers have access to a complete copy of the ledger, they can't trace anyone's real identity, the funds they own, or the transactions they have made.

This reversal of the traditional model leads to a reduction in the criticality of the information contained in the distributed ledger. Since security does not depend on the secrecy of the data, but on the protection of private keys, the distributed ledger is configured as an innovative and resistant solution for the management of sensitive information and critical applications.

5.3. Elimination of human error

In centralized systems, whoever manages the database or storage has almost absolute power over the system. Even if they operate in good faith, they can make mistakes that compromise the integrity of the data, with potentially disastrous consequences. In addition, this centralized power opens the door to possible abuse, allowing, for example, intentional manipulation of data for personal or partisan ends. This concentration of control represents a structural vulnerability, which requires a high level of trust in the operator, an aspect that is not always guaranteed.

In a blockchain, on the other hand, each node is autonomous and manages a complete copy of the ledger independently without being subordinate to a central authority. This distributed mechanism eliminates the risk of accidental or intentional errors by a single operator, since any change to the ledger made by the individual does not result in the modification of all the other copies stored on the other nodes: any modification proposed by a node is accepted if approved through a collective consensus involving the majority of the nodes in the network.

This distributed approach not only protects data integrity, but also reduces the reliance on trust in individuals or entities, creating a system where security is rooted in the architecture itself.

5.4. Is the distributed ledger therefore unassailable?

No, although very unlikely, there is a vulnerability called a **majority attack** or "51% attack".

If most of the nodes in the network were controlled by malicious actors, they could alter the ledger to their advantage. In this case, honest nodes would be faced with a choice: accept the illicit changes or leave the network, thus losing access to the registry.

However, the probability of a 51% attack decreases as the size of the network increases. With a few hundred nodes, such an attack becomes practically impossible because it would require enormous computational resources and extraordinary coordination.

5.5. Transaction validation

The distribution across multiple nodes makes the ledger resistant to failure, manipulation, and attacks, however, if a user simultaneously posts (using two nodes) two transactions that move the same funds to two different accounts, the nodes must decide which of the two transactions is valid and which to discard.

Since the Internet network to which the nodes are connected sends packets in sequence, inevitably each node will receive one of the two transactions before the other and therefore will consider the second invalid. However, being distributed all over the world, it can happen that one node receives transaction A first and then B, while another node receives transaction B first and then A.

Without a procedure that prevents this different view of reality by the nodes, there is a risk of misalignment of the copies of the ledger between the nodes of the network.

To solve this problem, special algorithms have been designed that allow the creation of "decentralized consensus".

This name immediately gives an idea of the goal: to allow each node of the network to understand autonomously, that is, without some form of centralized supervision system, which of the two transactions must be considered valid, regardless of the sequence in which it received them.

Inserting a centralized system into the blockchain would be the simplest solution, but as mentioned above, it would create a weakness that would nullify all the effort made to create a reliable ledger.

The absence of a centralized system is essential to prevent the storage problems solved by the distributed ledger from reappearing at the procedural level.

After several attempts, multiple methodologies have been found to achieve decentralized consensus, but they can be divided into two broad categories: leader-based and leaderless.

5.6. Consensus systems with leaders

Leader-based system-based methodologies require that a node in the network is periodically elected as a "validator".

Conceptually, trivializing decades of academic studies on this topic (I apologize, but the goal of this book is to make people understand, not be a scientific text), it is a bit like introducing a temporary centralized system.

Obviously, although chosen among nodes of the network with criteria that should guarantee the correctness of its work, the leader node remains a "trustless" node, so it can make mistakes or be corrected.

For this reason, its assertion of the validity of a transaction is not immediately considered valid. It will only be valid after other elected leaders have confirmed his work.

It is therefore a phased process in which several leaders confirm a transaction several times. Since the system is designed to make it unlikely that a leader can be elected several times consecutively, there is no one able to violate the procedure that produces consensus on the status of the ledger, i.e. on the correctness of the transactions it contains. The system is effectively decentralized

5.7. Leaderless systems

In leaderless systems, on the other hand, the procedure involves a vote on each transaction by nodes belonging to a "validation committee". Consensus is therefore obtained by the majority, even qualified, and the result of the vote immediately produces a definitive confirmation of the validity of a block.

The most famous and the first leaderless consensus algorithm to be created is called Byzantine Fault Tolerant.

Imagine an ancient empire, vast and powerful, with its capital besieged by a group of generals. The generals are stationed around the city and must decide how to attack: all together or retreat. Their strength lies in unity: if they attack in a coordinated way, they will win, but if some attack and others retreat, they will be defeated. But there's a catch: not all generals are loyal. Some may be traitors and spread false information to sabotage the common strategy.

This is the basis of the **Byzantine generals problem**, a classic dilemma of trust and coordination.

The generals decide to adopt a brilliant plan to solve the problem. Each general sends his own message to the others, declaring his intention: "I will attack" or "I will retreat." Each message is signed and verified to make sure it really comes from the sender. At this point, each general collects all the messages received and decides on the basis of the majority: if the majority says to attack, they attack; If most say to withdraw, they withdraw.

However, what happens if a traitorous general sends different messages to his colleagues? For example, they might say to one group, "Let's attack," and to another, "Let's withdraw." This is where a key principle of the BFT comes into play: **a decision is only made if a certain consensus threshold is reached**. This threshold, in most cases, is set at 66%+1 of participants. This means that even if up to a third of the generals were traitors, the loyal ones would still be able to make a coordinated decision.

In blockchains, each "general" is a node of the validator committee. To maintain the integrity of the ledger, each node must verify that a transaction is valid and then share its verification with the others. If enough nodes agree on validity, the transaction is added to the distributed ledger. Even if some nodes were compromised and tried to approve invalid blocks, the system remains safe as long as honest nodes are in the majority.

This consensus-making system is very robust. As the number of nodes increases, the probability that an attack could compromise 66%+1 of the nodes becomes smaller and smaller, to the point that it is impossible to breach the system.

However, as the number of validator nodes increases, so does the number of messages that must be exchanged to obtain the result. In a committee composed of N nodes, each node sends and receives N-1 messages, and this takes time and resources. In addition, the exchange of confirmation messages, for safety, is generally repeated several times.

This implies that the actual number of nodes in a BFT committee is typically limited to a dozen or so, making an attack on the majority less likely.

Over time, methods have been found that allow the performance of the protocol to be optimized, such as Practical BFT, and therefore today this system is used in many networks, such as the Ethereum network.

5.8. What exactly does the validator do?

The job of a validator node is to take all transactions created by users, verify that they are correct, put them in their own copy of the ledger, and publish the ledger update to the entire network. Invalid transactions are discarded.

A transaction is correct if:

- The data structure conforms to the protocol
- The digital signature is valid, i.e., it coincides with the one calculated using the public key indicated in the

transaction, from which the address from which the funds are withdrawn is derived.

- The fees paid are in accordance with those required by the network at the time of validation.

Note that validator nodes are not financial intermediaries because they do not directly participate in transactions between users and have no control over the funds transferred.

Their role is exclusively to validate and record transactions on the blockchain, ensuring the security and integrity of the system without affecting the content of the transactions themselves. Also note that, for simplicity and greater efficiency, every single transaction is validated but then a block of transactions is published at a time.

Publication takes place by connecting the new previous block, creating the chain from which the name blockchain derives, with the hash function.

By inserting the hash of the previous block into a new block, a timeline of blocks is created, and the entire chain is made unchangeable (we will see more about this aspect later when talking about the risk of "reog" of the chain).

The most famous consensus mechanism in the blockchain world is the system used by Bitcoin, known as **the Nakamoto Consensus**. It is named after its creator, the enigmatic Satoshi Nakamoto. This system has two main variants: **Proof of Work (PoW),** used by Bitcoin, and the more recent **Proof of Stake (PoS)** used in many other networks.

Proof of Work works as a sort of competition between the nodes of the network, called **miners**, to decide who will be the momentary leader with the right to add the next block of transactions to the blockchain (and get the corresponding reward).

5.9. Proof of Work

The competition of the validators of a PoW system begins with the selection of a set of transactions that each node wants to include in the next block. The node starts calculating the hash of the block repeatedly, changing a numeric parameter called a **nonce**. The goal is to find a hash that satisfies a specific condition: it must end with a sequence of zeros. The length of the sequence determines the difficulty, agreed upon by the network at that time. So blocks whose hash does not meet the minimum difficulty are considered invalid even if they contain only valid transactions.

Since there is no function to calculate the appropriate nonce given the block you want to validate, the only method you can use to win the competition is to modify the nonce and recalculate the hash and repeat until it meet the difficulty.

The difficulty is calculated periodically by each node with an algorithm that considers the average production interval of the blocks. Since they share the same ledger, all nodes infer the same new difficulty value. The goal is to keep the interval around a predefined value (for Bitcoin it is ten minutes). If higher, the difficulty is increased, if lower, it is decreased.

The first node that manages to find a valid hash becomes the temporary leader and gains the right to add the block to the chain. In return, he receives a **reward** in Bitcoin, along with the transaction fees included in the block.

In addition to choosing a leader, Proof of Work also creates a powerful deterrent against malicious behavior. If a leader tried to insert invalid transactions into a block and publish it, the other nodes in the network would reject it. The invalid block would be ignored and discarded, causing the malicious node to lose a total of the computational resources spent to compute it. This mechanism makes it too expensive and ineffective to try to violate the consensus protocol.

Over time, the competition to win the Proof of Work race has become increasingly intense. Miners began using specialized hardware, called **ASICs**, that could calculate billions of hashes per second. This has led to two main consequences:

- Cost growth: Specialized nodes have become very expensive and require high energy consumption.
- Reduction of the decentralization of power: only those with large financial resources can afford to compete, reducing the decentralization initially envisaged.

To address these limitations, a second variant of the Nakamoto consensus was born: Proof **of Stake (PoS).** This system works in a completely different way, eliminating competition based on computational power.

5.10. Proof of Stake

The idea behind PoS is that instead of investing capital in expensive ASICs and spending large amounts of money on energy, you can put the same amount as a guarantee that you will be playing the role of temporary leader properly.

PoS validators are required to put up a portion of their capital (usually in the form of network tokens) as **collateral as collateral**: if a validator attempted to publish a block containing invalid transactions, the network would punish them by destroying some or all of the collateral (a process called **slashing**) or redistributing it among other validators.

Thanks to this effort, the leader for each new block can be chosen randomly from a group of candidates or rotating nodes. In the first case, a network randomly chooses a validator, weighing the probability of being chosen based on the amount of capital locked. In the second case, validators are selected one after the other in a set order.

Proof of Stake consumes very little energy. No specialized hardware is needed, which allows anyone to participate. Finally, it reduces the concentration of power, as you can set a limit on a node's voting power regardless of the capital it controls.

6. Game Theory

Thanks to protocols that determine the behavior of nodes, the way transactions are produced, signed and disseminated on the network, a distributed ledger is secure and resistant to attacks.

The question arises: what prevents nodes from not respecting protocols by modifying the code of the node, trying to obtain illicit advantages?

Technically, there is nothing to prevent nodes from engaging in incorrect behavior that does not comply with protocols. Except that if they did, they would risk losing **Nash's equilibrium.**

Nash equilibrium is a central concept in Game Theory, a mathematical discipline that studies strategic decisions in situations where multiple participants, called "players," interact with each other. The theory analyzes how players can choose their strategies to maximize their own gain, considering the expected actions of others.

In particular, the Nash equilibrium describes a situation in which no player has an incentive to unilaterally change their strategy, provided that the other players maintain theirs. In other words, it is a state of stability in which each decision is optimal compared to the decisions of others. This principle applies in numerous fields, from economic theory to evolutionary biology to decentralized networks such as blockchain.

In the context of blockchains, the Nash equilibrium explains why participating nodes follow the shared protocol rather than trying to deviate from it. Incentive and penalty systems are designed to make rule-compliant behavior profitable, while the costs associated with deviations deter malicious behavior. This balance between costs and benefits creates a stable and secure system, in which cooperation between nodes ensures the functionality and integrity of the network.

For example, in the **Proof of Work (PoW)**-based consensus model, miners compete to add new blocks and receive token rewards. Attempting to deviate from the rules, such as mining invalid blocks, involves a high computational cost and a near-zero probability of success, making compliance with the rules the most rational strategy.

In **the Proof of Stake (PoS)** system, validators stake their tokens as collateral. If they follow the rules, they receive rewards. In the event of deviations, they risk losing their staked capital, a powerful disincentive that pushes them to comply with the protocol.

Byzantine Fault Tolerant (BFT) **models**, such as Tendermint, use a consensus between validator nodes to approve blocks. Severe penalties for malicious behavior, such as voting on invalid blocks, ensure that cooperation is increasingly beneficial.

Each blockchain defines its own incentive system based on specific needs, but the fundamental principle remains unchanged: ensuring that following the protocol's rules is economically and energetically more beneficial than deviating from them.

This principle also explains why decentralization cannot be sustained in a blockchain whose native token does not have sufficient value. In these cases, the potential gain from misconduct could easily outweigh the associated risk, leaving the entire network vulnerable. In the case of private or permissioned blockchains, where the native token is non-existent or has a purely symbolic value, the situation becomes even clearer. Without an economic value that incentivizes compliant behavior, nodes cannot be truly independent and must be trusted and permissioned to ensure the stability and security of the system. In such contexts, the responsibility for keeping the network compliant and secure falls on trust in the entities that control the nodes, rather than on economic incentives or decentralized mechanisms.

7. Blockchain attacks

We have already seen how some major security aspects, such as the risk that funds may be spent multiple times, are addressed and resolved with decentralized consensus protocols.

Let's now see how in reality this system is able to produce a much broader security perimeter than it seems at first glance, protecting not only the distributed ledger in the transaction recording phase, but also subsequently from other potentially destructive types of attacks.

7.1. Attempts to publish invalid blocks

The Nakamoto Consensus system, which underpins Bitcoin, is designed to create a blockchain that is as secure and valid as possible. In most cases, the system runs smoothly thanks to economic incentives: validators, or miners, are rewarded with rewards when they create valid blocks and are penalized, through a waste of resources, if they try to publish invalid blocks.

However, sometimes problems can occur. An invalid block, for example, could be published **by mistake or fraudulently**. In these cases, the system has a natural mechanism to deal with the situation: the fork.

A fork (literally "bifurcation") occurs when, diverging from a common point, two or more versions of the blockchain are formed. Imagine blockchain as a road that forks from a certain block onwards, there are two possible paths. This happens because a validator node has decided **not to link its block to the last block in the chain**, but to a previous block, which it considers valid, skipping the block it considers invalid.

This bifurcation is, in practice, a sort of voting system. Each block that is added to the chain represents not only a set of transactions, but also an expression of **trust and approval** towards all previous blocks. When a fork occurs, subsequent validators must choose which branch of the chain to vote on, thus deciding which version of the blockchain will become dominant.

The resolution of a fork is determined by the **longest chain**. In other words, the version of the blockchain that gets the most support from validators (i.e., that stretches the fastest) is considered the valid one. The least supported chain, which fails to grow, is automatically discarded.

Because of this mechanism, a transaction entered in a block cannot be considered immediately valid in the Nakamoto Consensus system. There is always a chance that a fork will occur, and the block will later be discarded. To ensure the security and irrevocability of transactions, it is necessary to wait for the chain to **stretch** by a certain number of blocks.

In the case of Bitcoin, the following are generally considered sufficient:

- **3 blocks** for small transactions.
- **6 blocks** for larger transactions.

This number is derived from statistical considerations based on network security. The Nakamoto Consensus makes it highly unlikely that a single miner (or malicious group) will be able to create **three or more consecutive blocks** fraudulently, without being overtaken by the main chain. Each new block added increases confidence in the validity of all previous blocks. After six blocks, the probability of a transaction being invalidated becomes virtually zero.

Forks can also be natural events; in fact it can happen that two valid blocks are published at the same time by two different miners.

This approach, while seemingly complex, has proven its effectiveness in keeping Bitcoin safe and reliable for over a decade.

The logic that drives the system is simple: the blockchain is not only a ledger of transactions, but also a ledger of trust. Each block is a collective statement that reinforces the validity of the entire chain, a brick in a castle built with mathematical precision.

7.2. reorg with Proof of Work

In addition to accidental or error-caused forks, there is another type of event that can change the structure of the blockchain, known as **a reorg** (short for "reorganization"). This term refers to a deep reorganization of the chain, often attempted with malicious intent to modify transactions already confirmed and consolidated in the blockchain.

To understand the reorg, let's imagine the blockchain as a tower of bricks, where each brick represents a block. Each new block is placed on top of the previous one, creating a robust and sequential structure. But what if someone tried to replace a brick at the base of the tower? This would not only change that single brick but would force you to rebuild the entire tower on top of it, since each block contains the hash of the previous block.

In a **reorg**, a malicious node attempts to publish an **alternative block** to a location far away in the chain, for example by replacing block 10 in a blockchain that has already reached block 20. This alternative block could contain significant changes, such as deleting or adding transactions, or even canceling a transfer of funds.

However, this is not simple: each block of the blockchain is linked to the previous one through its hash. Changing the contents of a block (e.g. block 10) changes its hash, making it incompatible with the next block (block 11), which contains the hash of the previous block. This cascading effect forces the attacker to reconstruct **all subsequent blocks**, finding new valid hashes for each of them. The difficulty of a reorg increases exponentially with the number of blocks that need to be rebuilt and this requires enormous computational power.

In addition, as the attacker attempts to reconstruct the modified blocks, the network continues to add new blocks to the original chain. To be successful, the attacker must not only catch up but also overcome the rate at which legitimate blocks are produced. This makes reorg almost impossible in networks with a high number of validators and high difficulty.

7.3. The reorg in a PoS system

While the nature and impact of a reorg will vary depending on the consensus system used, the basic principle remains the same for blockchains that adopt Proof of Stake consensus systems. However, such an attack requires malicious validators to accumulate a significant amount of capital to collateralize their work (stakes). Once this is achieved, they can try to reorganize the chain by presenting an alternative version that, while violating trust in the network, is technically sound.

This can happen, for example, when a group of validators work together to rewrite past blocks, or in situations where the network suffers from a period of low participation, reducing the threshold required to approve a block. Despite these possibilities, a reorg in a PoS system requires precise coordination and a significant investment. Validators who participate in such an attack almost certainly risk losing the capital at stake.

Ultimately, like PoW systems, the risk of a reorg in PoS systems is minimal, if not none, in large and highly participated networks.

7.4. The reorg in a BFT System

In a network based on BFT consensus mechanisms, reorg is an extremely unlikely event but not entirely impossible. A reorg in this context occurs when a group of validators attempts to reach an agreement to replace previous blocks with an alternative version. Unlike standard PoS systems, a BFT network imposes stringent requirements to approve a new block, making it very difficult to perform a reorg without being detected.

For a reorg to be successful in a BFT network, the attacker must compromise or control a significant portion of the validators, exceeding the minimum threshold required to reach consensus, which typically corresponds to two-thirds of honest validators. In addition, it must be able to coordinate compromised validators to create and sign alternative blocks without being detected. This level of coordination and control is extremely difficult to achieve in a well-designed network.

Although technically possible, reorg in a BFT system is highly unlikely. The network is structured to detect and block malicious behavior attempts in real time. In addition, honest validators are able to quickly identify a reorg attempt and activate security measures, such as excluding compromised validators, thus neutralizing the attack before it can cause significant damage.

7.5. Lack of network reaction to the reorg

An interesting aspect of **reorgs** is that all the other nodes in the network can, at least in theory, notice the attempt. This happens because the blocks involved in the contain data that has already been published and confirmed in the past. As a result, legitimate nodes in the network can easily identify that something unusual is happening.

But what exactly happens when nodes detect a reorg attempt? The answer is less immediate than one might think. Despite the ability to recognize an anomaly, blockchain protocols such as Bitcoin do not always have automatic **emergency procedures** to handle these events.

A reorg attempt may not generate an immediate or coordinated response from the network for several reasons. First, the consensus protocol is designed to be simple and efficient, and it doesn't distinguish between blocks published for the first time and blocks that seek to rearrange the chain. For the protocol, the chain considered valid is simply the longest one, i.e. the one with the highest number of valid blocks. This means that until the alternative blocks exceed the original chain in length, no particular action is taken.

Another reason is related to the decentralization and autonomy of the nodes. Each node operates independently and autonomously, choosing which chain to follow based on its length and validity. Although nodes can detect a reorg attempt, there is not and should not be a central authority or coordinated mechanism to respond to such attempts. The lack of a coordination mechanism protects the network from potential abuse or centralized manipulation, but implies that the response depends entirely on the individual decisions of the nodes.

Ultimately, the network takes a passive approach, letting the process unfold naturally and trusting in the inherent safety of the consensus mechanism to deter attempts at manipulation.

The lack of emergency mechanisms is both a strength and a potential weakness. On the one hand, it ensures that the system remains simple, decentralized, and resistant to arbitrary intervention. On the other hand, it means that the network relies completely on **statistics** and the **distribution of computational resources** to prevent attacks.

So, in theory, if an attacker were powerful and determined enough, they could exploit this lack of immediate response to complete a deep reorg, potentially causing severe economic and reputational damage to the network. But this is highly unlikely.

7.6. The legitimate reorg

Although the reorg is generally a hostile event aimed at illicitly altering the history of the registry with the aim of stealing funds, there is a case in which the reorg can be considered legitimate. That's what happened to fix the hack of "The DAO," a decentralized smart contract-based application on the Ethereum network.

In 2016, a hacker exploited a vulnerability in The DAO's code, stealing around $60 million in Ether. This event sparked a heated debate within the Ethereum community. Some argued that the principle of blockchain immutability should be preserved, allowing theft to remain recorded in the chain. Others, however, considered it necessary to intervene to return the stolen funds to their rightful owners.

The solution adopted was to perform a deliberate reorg of the blockchain, creating a new version of the chain that ignored transactions related to theft. This reorg marked the birth of a split in the network: the updated version became Ethereum (ETH), while the original version, which remained unchanged, continued to operate under the name Ethereum Classic (ETC).

The episode of The DAO remains a case in point, not only for the use of a reorg as a resolution tool, but also for the ethical and philosophical debate it generated, posing fundamental questions about the balance between immutability and justice in the context of blockchains.

The DAO episode also highlighted the importance of **network governance**, highlighting how collective decisions can impact the direction of a blockchain. Governance, which should ideally reflect the principles of decentralization, often finds itself having to balance conflicting interests, such as respecting the immutability of the ledger and the need to resolve extraordinary events that undermine trust in the network.

Blockchain governance is a fascinating topic that would deserve an entire book, so I won't go into it further for now, but searching the net you will certainly find a lot of in-depth content.

8. The costs of blockchain

While blockchains offer a revolutionary model of security and transparency, they are not without their costs. Cost can be analyzed in various aspects, including energy costs, transaction fees, infrastructure costs, and scalability costs. Understanding these elements is crucial for assessing the sustainability and effectiveness of a blockchain system, whether public or private.

8.1. Energy Costs

One of the most talked about aspects of blockchains is energy consumption, especially for those based on consensus algorithms such as **Proof of Work (PoW).** Blockchains such as Bitcoin and Ethereum (until the transition to Proof of Stake) use PoW. This competition involves the use of a huge amount of electricity.

According to recent estimates, the Bitcoin network consumes as much energy as entire nations such as Argentina or the Netherlands. This energy cost raises both economic and environmental concerns, prompting the development of alternative consensus algorithms, such as **Proof of Stake (PoS)** or **Proof of Authority (PoA),** which require a fraction of the energy needed for PoW.

8.2. Transaction fees or commissions

Each transaction on the blockchain involves a cost, generally called a **transaction fee** or commission. This cost varies greatly depending on the network and the level of congestion. On blockchains like Ethereum, transaction fees are affected by the demand for computational resources, as complex operations require more **gas**.

Gas is a measure that represents the amount of computational work required to perform a given operation on the blockchain. Every operation, whether it's transferring tokens, interacting with a smart contract, or performing complex calculations, has a gas cost that depends on its complexity. For example, a simple ETH transfer transaction requires less gas than running a smart contract that processes data or creates other transactions.

The actual cost of a transaction is calculated by multiplying the **price of gas** (expressed in Gwei, a fraction of ETH) by the amount of gas required by the operation (**gas limit**). During periods of high demand, the price of gas rises as users compete to have their transactions included in blocks, which have a cumulative maximum gas limit. This dynamic mechanism ensures that validators on the network are adequately incentivized to include transactions in blocks.

A concrete example occurred during the NFT and **DeFi** boom, when Ethereum's fees reached very high levels. Operations that normally required a few dollars in gas have come to cost tens or hundreds of dollars, making the network less accessible for applications that rely on microtransactions.

In response to these issues, Ethereum has introduced improvements such as **EIP-1559**, which redesigned the fee system by introducing a **base fee** (a variable minimum fee for each transaction) and a **burning mechanism** that destroys a portion of the gas paid, reducing the overall supply of ETH and improving the economic sustainability of the system.

For example, during periods of high activity, such as the **NFT** boom of 2021, fees on Ethereum peaked at tens or hundreds of dollars per single transaction, making the network inaccessible for applications that need microtransactions. Alternative blockchains, such as Binance Smart Chain or Polygon, offer significantly lower fees, attracting users looking for cheaper solutions.

8.3. Others costs

In addition to the costs related to fees and energy consumption of Proof of Work (PoW), blockchains also involve significant expenses for technological infrastructure, both on the network and user side. Node management is one of the main cost items. Each node in the network must store the entire blockchain ledger, which can grow to a considerable size as the network grows. Managing "full nodes" – nodes that hold the entire registry – requires advanced hardware, large storage capacities, and constant maintenance to ensure network reliability and operation.

Another critical aspect is the development and maintenance of blockchain-based applications, such as smart contracts or DApps. Creating these solutions requires highly specialized development teams and meticulous attention to security. A single error in a smart contract code can have serious consequences, such as financial losses or malfunctions, and therefore requires additional investment in fixes and updates. These costs highlight how blockchain adoption involves economic and technical challenges that go beyond transactional fees and direct energy consumption.

9. Blockchain performance

Satoshi Nakamoto**'s initial goal** was to create a decentralized, non-intermediated payment system capable of supporting the entire volume of global monetary exchanges. However, from a performance perspective, the **Bitcoin** network is far from achieving this ambition. Its architecture, designed primarily to ensure security and immutability, imposes significant limits on the speed and processing capacity of transactions.

The Bitcoin network works by generating a new block every 10 minutes or so, although the time may vary slightly based on network conditions. Each block contains a limited number of transactions, typically between **2,000 and 4,000**, depending on their complexity.

This means that Bitcoin can process on average:

2-4 transactions per second (TPS). In comparison, a global payment system like Visa can process up to **24,000 TPS** at peak times.

In addition, to ensure that a transaction is confirmed definitively, it is necessary to wait for the blockchain to stretch by at least 3 successive blocks. This is to reduce the risk of forks, but it implies that a Bitcoin transaction requires a confirmation time of **20-30 minutes**. This makes the network unsuitable for everyday uses, such as online payments or in-store purchases, where speed is critical.

Bitcoin's financial success has inspired many developers to create alternative blockchains or improvements that address its limitations in scalability and speed.

Let's look at some of the most important networks and their performance:

Ethereum (ETH):
> TPS: **15-30 TPS** (Ethereum 1.0); with the upgrade to **Ethereum 2.0**, which uses Proof of Stake, a significant increase is expected, potentially up to **100,000 TPS** thanks to sharding (which I discuss in the next chapter).
>
> Confirmation time: **15-30 seconds per block**, but for a complete finality it takes several minutes.

According to the Sun:
> TPS: **65,000 theoretical TPS** , with actual performance around **4,000-6,000 TPS**.
>
> Confirmation time: Approximately **2.5 seconds per block**, making it one of the fastest networks for transaction-intensive applications.

Cardano (ADA):
> TPS: Approximately **250 TPS** with the Ouroboros protocol; future scalability expected via Hydra, which could theoretically bring the network to over **1 million TPS**.
>
> Confirmation time: **20-30 seconds**.

Ripple (XRP):
> TPS: **1,500 TPS**, with the ability to scale up to **50,000 TPS** for institutional uses.

Confirmation time: about **3-5 seconds**, making it very competitive for cross-border payments.

Palakadat (Dat):

TPS: **1,000 TPS** on current parachains, with the ability to scale further.

Confirmation time: **6 seconds per block.**

Avalanche (Avex):

TPS: Fino a **4.500 TPS**.

Confirmation time: about **1 second**, thanks to its innovative Avalanche Consensus protocol.

Algorand (ALGO):

TPS: 6,000 TPS.

Confirmation time: about **4.5 seconds**, ideal for fast financial applications.

IOTA 2.0 Rebased (IOTA)

TPS: oltre **50.000 TPS**

Confirmation time: approx. 0.5 seconds ideal for banking and industrial applications

9.1. Is it possible to increase the performance of blockchains?

Maintaining a minimum time interval between the publication of two blocks is essential to ensure the wide participation of nodes in the network.

However, this solution introduces a significant side effect: it makes the entire system **synchronous**, with all nodes operating at the same time rate. According to the **FLP theorem** (Fischer, Lynch and Paterson), a synchronous system has inherent limitations in the handling of Byzantine failures: too long an interval can slow down the entire network, while too short an interval could compromise the stability and participation of slower nodes.

To mitigate this limitation, two fundamental parameters can be acted upon: security and decentralization. One possibility is to introduce rules in the consensus protocol that shorten verification procedures for certain types of transactions, such as those that move little value. This approach improves performance by reducing the computational load for these transactions, but inevitably introduces an element of risk to the security of the system. In certain contexts, where the impact of a possible error or attack is limited, this exception may be acceptable.

Another option to increase performance is to limit the number of validators and adopt a Byzantine Fault Tolerance (BFT) consensus model. With fewer validators, decision-making becomes faster, and consensus can be reached in significantly less time. However, this solution reduces the decentralization of the network and increases the risk that a group of malicious nodes could gain control, compromising the integrity of the system.

These trade-offs are at the heart of the **blockchain trilemma**, a principle that states that it is not possible to simultaneously improve all three fundamental properties of a blockchain — security, scalability, and decentralization. Every improvement in one dimension inevitably involves a sacrifice in the others.

However, there is another way to address this challenge: redesigning the blockchain so that nodes operate **asynchronously**. In an asynchronous system, nodes do not need to be rigidly synchronized. This approach significantly reduces time dependency as a critical factor, allowing nodes to process transactions at varying speeds and improving overall scalability without compromising security.

To make a blockchain asynchronous, it is necessary to rethink the traditional structure of the ledger, organized as a sequential chain of blocks. In an asynchronous system, it is critical to allow validators to insert multiple blocks simultaneously, thus eliminating the need for strict sequencing. To achieve this flexibility, the blocks must be concatenated using a different structure: a **Directed Acyclic Graph** (DAG).

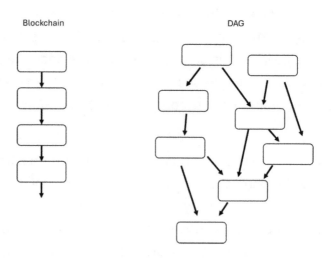

A DAG allows multiple blocks to be added to the structure at the same time, ensuring that data remains structured in a consistent and auditable manner. In this configuration, the blocks do not follow a strictly ordered timeline, but are organized in a configuration in which each block can have multiple predecessors, as long as no loops are created within the graph.

This innovation introduces new challenges, particularly the management of conflicting transactions. In fact, when multiple blocks are added simultaneously, it can happen that two blocks include mutually exclusive transactions, such as two moves of the same balance from the same account.

To resolve these conflicts, a new consensus system designed specifically for DAGs is needed. This system must be able to identify and resolve transaction conflicts quickly and reliably, ensuring that the final ledger remains consistent and secure. Several DAG-based blockchains, such as **IOTA, Avalanche**, and **SUI,** have developed innovative solutions to address these issues, demonstrating that asynchronous mode can be a game-changer in the scalability and efficiency of distributed networks.

9.2. New DAG-based consensus models

Among the most recent and promising proposals, the **Narwhal** and **Bullshark** protocols are emerging as innovative solutions to improve data management and transaction efficiency in decentralized networks.

As we have seen, in traditional protocols, consensus is produced on a linear sequence of blocks that is built by nodes that compete or collaborate to propose and validate successive blocks. This approach, while ensuring security and immutability, introduces significant bottlenecks from which performance limits arise. Latency in block propagation and the need to manage the risk of forks reduce the speed and efficiency of the system, making it difficult to scale networks for global use.

An alternative approach is to organize the ledger into blocks connected to several previous blocks, with the only constraint of creating a Direct Acyclic Graph (DAG), i.e. that no links are made that create closed paths.

This approach allows multiple nodes to create a block at the same time, a bit like if they were creating a fork, but in reality, both blocks are valid and subsequent ones will be able to approve both by connecting to them.

On the basis of this new organizational model of the blocks, new models of consensus have been created.

One of the most critical challenges for blockchains is ensuring that all nodes in the network have access to the data needed to validate a block, even in the face of attacks or outages.

Narwhal introduces an innovative architecture that separates data **availability** from **actual consent**. Instead of immediately focusing on choosing the next block, Narwhal first focuses on ensuring that all the required data is available and replicated across the network. This process takes place through a directed acyclic graph structure, in which blocks are stored securely and in parallel.

This separation eliminates data propagation bottlenecks, significantly improving network resiliency and scalability. Narwhal then integrates with various consensus protocols to finalize blocks, while maintaining the immutability and security of the blockchain.

Bullshark is a protocol that builds on top of Narwhal, using the data already organized in the DAG to optimize the consensus process. Unlike traditional protocols, Bullshark doesn't just pick one block at a time, it leverages the DAG structure to efficiently select valid blocks and finalize them sequentially.

The combination of Narwhal and Bullshark allows you to achieve deterministic **finality** with extremely low latency, ensuring that transactions are considered final in seconds. In addition, Bullshark uses advanced validation mechanisms to reduce the risk of attacks, even in adverse network conditions.

Experimentally, these protocols have been shown to handle more than 150,000 transactions per second, with 3 – 4 seconds of maximum waiting for final confirmation.

9.3. Sharding e Layer 2

Another approach to overcoming the blockchain trilemma without overly sacrificing security or decentralization is to adopt **sharding**.

Derived from the world of distributed databases, sharding has been adapted to blockchains to allow the handling of an increasing number of transactions, while ensuring operational efficiency and high performance.

The principle of sharding is to divide the network into smaller partitions, called shards. Each shard operates as an autonomous mini-network, processing a subset of transactions and storing a portion of the global ledger. This approach allows the workload to be distributed among different nodes, reducing the need for each node to process and store the entire blockchain. In other words, rather than forcing all nodes to verify each transaction, sharding allows them to take care of only a specific portion of the work.

Technically, sharding is divided into two main dimensions. The first is transaction sharding, where each shard processes a specific set of transactions, working in parallel with the other shards. The second is state sharding, which involves splitting blockchain data, such as balances and smart contracts, between shards. To maintain global consistency, shards must communicate with each other through a coordination mechanism that is often centralized in a main chain, called a beacon chain.

The benefits of sharding are many. It significantly increases the scalability of the network, allowing thousands or even millions of transactions to be processed per second, as the shards work in parallel. It also reduces the load on individual nodes, making it more accessible to participate in the network. This approach promotes greater decentralization, as you don't need to have highly specialized hardware to help make the blockchain work.

However, sharding is not without its challenges. One of the main ones is cross-shard communication, known as cross-shard communication. Transactions involving multiple shards require an exchange of information between the different partitions, which can introduce complexity and slowdowns. Another difficulty is related to security: if a shard is compromised, the data and transactions it contains can be vulnerable. This issue requires robust consensus mechanisms to protect each shard. Finally, ensuring global consistency is a complex technical challenge, especially on large decentralized networks, as shards must constantly synchronize.

Some blockchains have adopted sharding to improve their performance. Ethereum 2.0, for example, is implementing sharding that divides the network into sixty-four shards, greatly increasing transaction processing capacity. Polkadot uses a similar approach with parachains, where each shard operates semi-independently but is coordinated by the central relay chain. NEAR Protocol has developed dynamic sharding, where the number of shards can be increased or reduced based on network demand, thus optimizing available resources. Zilliqa has also stood out for its implementation of sharding, achieving high throughputs thanks to the splitting of transactions.

Sharding is an effective response to the scalability limitations of traditional blockchains. Despite the technical challenges it brings, its potential to significantly increase the performance of networks makes it one of the most promising solutions for the future of blockchains. Its application continues to evolve, and technological advances are helping to overcome implementation difficulties, making sharding increasingly central to the landscape of distributed technologies.

9.4. Layer 2: Off-chain scalability

Another widely used solution to multiply the performance of the blockchain is **Layer 2** (or L2).

They represent one of the most effective approaches to address the problem of scalability in blockchains, without compromising security and decentralization. Unlike methods that directly change the functioning of the main blockchain (Layer 1), L2 solutions operate on top of it, moving a significant portion of transaction processing off the main chain. This allows the security and immutability of the underlying blockchain to be maintained, while relieving its burden.

The core principle of Layer 2 solutions is to manage transactions off-chain, processing them in a parallel environment and recording only the final results on the main blockchain, usually in the form of a single aggregated transaction. This approach not only increases the network's ability to handle transactions, but it significantly reduces processing costs and time.

A classic example of Layer 2 is the **Lightning Network**, which is designed for Bitcoin. The Lightning Network allows you to open a payment channel between two users, through which numerous two-way transactions can be made. Only the opening and closing of the channel are recorded on the main blockchain, while intermediate transactions remain off-chain. This system is particularly useful for microtransactions, where transaction costs on the main blockchain would be too high.

Another popular approach in the blockchain world is rollups, which are mainly used on Ethereum. Rollups process thousands of off-chain transactions and send only a summary to the main blockchain, along with cryptographic proof that ensures the validity of transactions. Rollups can be of two main types: **Optimistic Rollups**, which assume that transactions are valid unless disputed, and **ZK Rollups** (Zero-Knowledge Rollups), which use zero-knowledge proofs to prove the validity of transactions in a secure and efficient manner.

Layer 2 solutions offer many benefits. First, they drastically improve the scalability of the network, allowing it to handle thousands of transactions per second without overloading the main blockchain. They also reduce transaction costs, as they move much of the processing off-chain, where resources are less expensive. Another significant advantage is speed: Layer 2 transactions are usually confirmed almost instantly, improving the user experience.

However, Layer 2 solutions present some challenges. One of the main ones is their technical complexity, which requires advanced protocols and additional infrastructure to operate securely. In addition, Layer 2 security is highly dependent on the main blockchain. While data is often compressed and aggregated, any vulnerabilities in the underlying blockchain could compromise the integrity of the entire system. Finally, compatibility between different Layer 2 solutions can be an issue, as each implementation is often optimized for a specific blockchain or use case.

In the current landscape, many blockchains are adopting Layer 2 solutions to improve their performance. In addition to the Lightning Network on Bitcoin and rollups on Ethereum, there are other successful implementations. Polygon, for example, is a Layer 2 platform that uses sidechains to improve Ethereum's scalability, making it possible to process thousands of transactions with reduced costs. Arbitrum and Optimism are examples of optimistic rollups on Ethereum, offering high throughput and low fees. StarkNet, on the other hand, is a solution based on ZK Rollups that stands out for its use of zero-knowledge proofs, ensuring advanced security.

As these technologies continue to evolve, Layer 2 will become increasingly central to the future of blockchains, allowing them to meet the demands of large-scale adoption.

10. Virtual Machine e Smart Contract

Virtual Machines (VMs) represent one of the most significant innovations in the blockchain landscape. They constitute the virtual environment in which smart contracts are executed, enabling automation, programmability, and interoperability within a decentralized network. Their introduction transformed blockchains from simple transaction recording systems to dynamic platforms capable of supporting decentralized applications (dApps) and a wide range of digital services.

Note that, despite their name, smart contracts do not implicitly have legal value equivalent to that of a traditional contract, such as a purchase and sale contract. This happens because the parties involved, identified through a public key or an address, are not necessarily traceable to specific identities. In the legal field, for a contract to be valid, it is necessary that the parties are identifiable in a certain and unambiguous way, so as to guarantee their legal capacity to act and responsibility for the obligations assumed.

The absence of identification of the parties in smart contracts also leads to the loss of the **principle of non-enforceability against third parties**, which is essential to give full legal validity to an agreement. This principle ensures that the rights and obligations arising from a contract are recognized not only between the parties, but also vis-à-vis external parties. In smart contracts, on the other hand, the lack of verifiable association between cryptographic keys and legal identities makes it impossible to enforce the agreement against third parties, limiting the effectiveness of the contract in a traditional legal context.

To fill this gap, it is necessary to integrate smart contracts with certified digital identification systems, such as **Decentralized Identifiers (DIDs),** which allow a blockchain address to be associated with a legally recognized entity. See the specific chapter.

10.1. The VM your Ethereum

The first blockchain to integrate a Virtual Machine was **Ethereum,** which was launched in 2015. The idea behind Ethereum was simple but revolutionary: to allow users to write custom programs — so-called smart contracts — and run them directly on the blockchain. To accomplish this, Ethereum developers created the **Ethereum Virtual Machine** (EVM), a universal runtime environment in which any compatible program can be executed.

The EVM was designed to be a Turing-complete virtual machine, capable of running any computable program, as long as you have sufficient resources. The goal was to create a decentralized system that would allow complex processes to be automated without the need for intermediaries, thus paving the way for new business models and innovative applications.

The **Ethereum Virtual Machine** has become a de facto standard for many blockchains. Its compatibility and vast ecosystem of tools and libraries have led numerous projects to integrate EVM as part of their technology stack. Networks such as **Binance Smart Chain (BSC), Polygon, Avalanche, Fantom, Optimism,** and many others support EVM, allowing developers to use Solidity and migrate decentralized applications between different blockchains with ease.

This interoperability has created a network effect, accelerating the adoption of EVM-compatible blockchains and reinforcing the importance of open standards in the industry. However, the reliance on EVM has also brought some limitations, particularly with regard to security and flexibility, prompting the creation of new Virtual Machine models.

10.2. Smart contract

Smart **contracts** are programs that run automatically when the conditions set by the code are met. For example, you can trigger a smart contract feature with a transaction that contains specific metadata.

Smart contracts are written in a specific programming language that produces executable code that is compatible with the Virtual Machine of the blockchain on which they operate. In the case of Ethereum, the most widely used language is **Solidity**.

Solidity allows developers to write contracts that manage digital assets, execute exchanges, govern decentralized autonomous organizations (DAOs), and much more. Smart contracts, once deployed on the blockchain, become immutable and completely autonomous: no one can prevent a smart contract from being activated, no one can change the code that is stored in the ledger through a transaction, and of course no one can delete a smart contract. The only exception to this total decentralization is the possibility given to the person who published the smart contract to publish a new version. This normally happens to add functionality or fix errors in the code. In any case, the smart contract identifier changes, so the user is inevitably aware that something has been changed. To prevent two versions of the smart contract from being accessible at the same time, each smart contract typically contains a self-destruct function that can be activated by its administrator. This feature eliminates the executable code of the smart contract from the blockchain but not the transactions. This prevents you from activating the smart contract again but does not prevent you from analyzing the history of its activations.

Thanks to smart contracts, blockchains have gone from being simple distributed ledgers to programmable platforms, capable of managing complex interactions between users, systems and applications.

10.3. La Move Virtual Machine

One of the most recent answers to EVM challenges is the **Move Virtual Machine (Move VM),** which was originally introduced by Facebook's blockchain project Libra (later cancelled), and later adopted by other networks such as **Aptos, Sui** and **IOTA.**

Move has been designed with a specific focus on safety, modularity and efficiency.

Move smart contracts are written in Rust, a very robust C-like language.

Unlike EVM, Move uses an asset-based model, where digital assets are treated as objects with well-defined properties. This approach significantly reduces the risk of common smart contract development errors, such as the re-entry bug, which has caused major security issues in many Ethereum-based applications.

The Move VM also offers flexibility and performance benefits. Its programming language, also called **Move**, is designed to be more intuitive and less error-prone than Solidity. Additionally, Move allows developers to create modular, reusable contracts, improving the efficiency of the development process.

10.4. Execution and effects of smart contracts

Smart contracts are created by compiling source code written in a specific language, such as **Solidity** or **Move**, and publishing the executable to the blockchain. This is done through a transaction sent to an address that is generally derived directly from the code itself, ensuring a unique and immutable link between the address and the smart contract.

Like a normal computer program, a smart contract can define variables to store data and functions that describe the programmed behavior. Once published on the blockchain, it is possible to interact with the smart contract by calling its functions through transactions sent to the associated address. Each function can receive specific parameters, which determine the execution of the code contained in the smart contract.

The validator nodes, in the process of validating these transactions, upload the smart contract code to their **Virtual Machine (VM).** During execution, smart contract code can change internal variables or create new transactions that move tokens or interact with other smart contracts. Validators, once the code is executed, include a new version of the state associated with the smart contract in the block, updating the values of the variables and recording any transactions generated.

A key aspect of smart contracts is that they do not need to sign the transactions they generate. This is because the execution of the smart contract takes place within the block validation process, under the supervision of the validator nodes. Since blocks created by validators are considered valid by definition (unless errors are detected during consensus), transactions generated by smart contracts included in those blocks are also automatically considered valid.

In the event that the execution of the smart contract produces an incorrect result or inconsistent with the rules of the protocol, the block containing such execution would be rejected by the network through a fork. As a result, any transactions resulting from the execution of the smart contract in that block would also be voided, preserving the integrity of the network and ensuring that only valid and consistent states are recorded in the blockchain. This mechanism makes smart contracts an essential element for automating processes and ensuring transparency and security in decentralized applications.

A basic example of the use of a smart contract is a decentralized counter on a public blockchain that counts the number of occurrences of events that trigger it. The event can be of any type, detected by a control system that activates the smart contract to track it. This counter keeps track of how many times it is called and returns the total number of activations. Each time a user interacts with the contract, sending a transaction, the counter increments its value by one and updates the status on the blockchain. The new value is visible to everyone, guaranteeing transparency and immutability.

This counter is completely decentralized. It is not controlled by any organization and operates autonomously following the rules defined in its code. Any change to the value of the meter is done through transactions recorded on the blockchain, which ensures that there is no manipulation.

Another important benefit is resilience. Because the counter is distributed over a network of nodes, it does not depend on the reliability of a single server. Even in the event of failures or cyberattacks on some nodes, the meter will continue to operate without interruption. Additionally, thanks to the public nature of the blockchain, anyone can verify meter activity and check that the value is correct.

This type of counter is particularly useful in scenarios where transparency and trust are key. For example, it could be used to count logins to a service or attendance at an event, ensuring that the count cannot be altered. However, the use of a blockchain introduces costs and delays due to transactions, making it less suitable for situations that require frequent or high-speed updates.

Another important use of smart contracts is the ability to create **tokens**, which represent digital or physical assets and can be traded on the blockchain. Through smart contracts, it is possible to define the rules of operation of a token, such as the maximum number of units available, the mode of transfer, any rights associated with possession and the conditions for the creation or destruction of the tokens themselves.

In the Ethereum ecosystem, tokens follow specific standards known as **ERC** (Ethereum Request for Comments). ERCs are protocols that define the rules that a smart contract must comply with to create a token that is compatible with Ethereum's infrastructure, including wallets, exchanges, and decentralized applications. For example, **ERC-20** is the most common standard for fungible tokens, such as cryptocurrencies, where each unit has the same value and can be exchanged for another identical one. **ERC-721**, on the other hand, is the standard for **Non-Fungible Tokens (NFTs),** which represent unique and non-interchangeable digital assets, such as digital artwork or collectibles.

These tokens find application in numerous industries, including decentralized finance (DeFi), blockchain gaming, digital art, and loyalty programs. Thanks to smart contracts and standards such as ERCs, the management and exchange of tokens become transparent, secure, and automated, eliminating the need for intermediaries.

The standardization introduced by the ERCs has made Ethereum the leader in the issuance and management of tokens, allowing for rapid innovation and interoperability between projects. This has enabled the tokenization of a wide range of assets, from physical assets such as real estate or luxury items to intangible assets such as copyrights, licenses, or exclusive access to services, paving the way for new economic and ownership models.

10.5. Bridges amd the wrapped Tokens

Because the Ethereum Virtual Machine (EVM) is compatible with the nodes of many blockchains, ERC standards have established themselves as global standards in the blockchain industry. This interoperability allows tokens to be moved virtually between different blockchains, while maintaining their functionality and compliance with the same protocols.

This is done through mechanisms such as bridges, which use smart contracts to connect different networks. Bridges allow users to transfer tokens from one blockchain to another without losing control over their value. The process involves locking the original tokens in a smart contract on the source blockchain and generating an equivalent, known as a wrapped token, on the destination blockchain. Smart contracts ensure that the total number of tokens remains constant and that value is preserved, synchronizing operations between the two networks in a secure and transparent manner.

These wrapped tokens, which represent the value of the original tokens, can be used on the target blockchain as if they were native. At the time of "returning" to the source blockchain, the smart contracts involved in the bridge are responsible for "unlocking" the original tokens and destroying the wrapped token, maintaining the balance between the two networks.

Another approach to moving tokens between blockchains is the adoption of multi-chain standards, such as those introduced by Polygon or Avalanche, which use advanced smart contracts to manage direct transfers between EVM-compatible blockchains. These standards eliminate the need for external bridges and improve transfer efficiency.

10.6. The Initial Coin Offering

The ability to create tokens has paved the way for a new way of raising funds to fund projects, through a process known as **Initial Coin Offering (ICO).** This mechanism has revolutionized the world of decentralized finance, allowing entrepreneurs to issue tokens to represent rights, shares, or utilities related to their projects, and investors to easily participate in innovative initiatives. The peak of ICOs came in

2017, a year when thousands of projects used this method to raise capital, attracting billions of dollars in investment.

The process of an ICO is based on smart contracts that automate the creation and distribution of tokens. Investors send cryptocurrencies, such as Ether or Bitcoin, to a smart contract that, in return, generates and sends the corresponding tokens to investors' addresses. This system ensures transparency and immediate allocation of tokens, eliminating the need for traditional intermediaries.

ICOs have led to a democratization of funding, allowing anyone in the world, with an internet connection, to invest in startups and blockchain projects. However, the phenomenon also had downsides. The absence of regulation has allowed fraudulent or poor-quality projects to emerge, leading many investors to lose their funds. This prompted several authorities to intervene, introducing regulations to protect investors and ensure greater transparency.

Despite the decline in ICOs after 2018, due to a combination of speculative bubbles and new regulations, the concept has continued to evolve. More structured forms of fundraising, such as **Security Token Offerings (STOs)** and **Initial Exchange Offerings (IEOs),** have replaced traditional ICOs, integrating greater regulatory compliance and investor protection mechanisms. In parallel, the emergence of **decentralized finance (DeFi)** has led to new ways of fundraising, such as **Initial DEX Offerings (IDOs),** which leverage decentralized platforms to distribute tokens in an even more transparent and democratic way.

The ICO was a historic moment for the blockchain industry, demonstrating the potential of tokens as an innovative financial tool. While the traditional model has been overtaken by more regulated approaches, its legacy lives on through the evolutions that continue to redefine the way projects and startups raise funds in the digital world.

11. The Blockchain Tokenomics

Tokenomics refers to the form of economy of a blockchain that regulates tokens, establishing their creation, distribution and use. Tokenomics is one of the key elements in ensuring the functioning and sustainability of a decentralized network. It determines not only the economic value of the token, but also the level of participation in the network and, consequently, its security. In a decentralized system, the link between the token's value and participant behavior is crucial: a well-designed token incentivizes active participation, ensuring the resilience and reliability of the network.

There are two main types of tokens in relation to tokenomics: **cryptocurrencies** and **tokenized assets**. Cryptocurrencies, such as Bitcoin, are not issued by an identifiable entity. They are born from a decentralized protocol and follow mathematical and cryptographic rules for their creation and distribution. Tokenized **assets**, on the other hand, represent values or rights issued by an identifiable entity, such as a company, and are linked to the development project of a specific blockchain. This distinction profoundly influences the tokenomics of the respective networks.

11.1. Bitcoin Tokenomics

Bitcoin is the first and most well-known example of a cryptocurrency, with a tokenomics based on a **Proof of Work (PoW)** mechanism. Bitcoins are created through a process known as **mining**, in which miners compete to solve complex cryptographic problems and add blocks to the blockchain. For each validated block, miners receive a Bitcoin reward, which is halved every four years in a process called **halving**.

This system creates a direct link between the value of the token and the security of the network. Because Bitcoin's value is high, miners are incentivized to invest in hardware and power consumption to participate in mining. Increasing computational difficulty increases network security, making it extremely difficult for an attacker to gain control of 51% of the computational power and compromise the system. In addition, the token's programmed scarcity (with a maximum limit of 21 million units) preserves its value over time, making Bitcoin a store of value and a secure and independent means of payment.

11.2. Ethereum Tokenomics

Ethereum is an example of a versatile tokenomics, evolving from a PoW-based model to a **Proof of Stake (PoS)**-based one with the introduction of Ethereum 2.0. In this model, users can participate in the security of the network by depositing a minimum amount of **32 ETH,** becoming validators. This process, known as **staking**, rewards users with new ETH issuance in proportion to their contribution.

Ethereum tokenomics also stands out for its use as **a gas**, which is required to pay for transaction fees and smart contract executions. This link between ETH and the practical use of the network creates a constant demand, affecting the value of the token. With the **EIP-1559** upgrade, Ethereum introduced a **burning** mechanism, where a portion of the fees are destroyed, reducing the total supply of ETH and introducing deflationary pressure. This approach incentivizes participation in the network, improves the economic sustainability of the system, and further ties the value of the token to the activity of the blockchain.

12. Exchanges

Exchanges are essential platforms in the cryptocurrency landscape, as they allow users to buy, sell, and trade digital assets such as Bitcoin, Ethereum, and thousands of other tokens. These tools have evolved rapidly, adopting different models to meet the needs of security, decentralization, and ease of use. They are mainly distinguished into **CEX** (Centralized Exchange) and **DEX** (Decentralized Exchange), each with specific features, advantages, and limitations.

Exchanges are indispensable platforms in the cryptocurrency ecosystem, as they allow users to buy, sell, and trade digital assets such as Bitcoin, Ethereum, and thousands of other tokens. They are mainly divided into two categories: **centralized exchanges (CEXs)** and **decentralized exchanges (DEXs),** each with distinctive features and leading platforms that have shaped the industry.

12.1. Centralized Exchange (CEX)

Centralized exchanges, or **CEXs**, are platforms operated by centralized entities that facilitate cryptocurrency trading. The fact that they are centralized, of course, conflicts with all the logic of decentralization of blockchains, however when they were activated, it was unimaginable to implement the services they offer directly on the blockchain.

Among the most well-known globally are **Binance**, the largest by trading volume, **Coinbase**, popular for its ease of use and regulated approach, and **Kraken**, appreciated for its security and advanced services. Other notable names include **Bitfinex**, known for high liquidity, and **Bybit**, a high-growth derivatives trading platform.

In CEXs, users deposit funds to an exchange address and submit buy or sell orders through a web application, where orders are automatically matched. These exchanges offer a wide range of services, including margin trading, futures, staking, and even payment cards linked to users' wallets.

The main advantages of CEXs are ease of use, high liquidity, and speed of transactions. However, their centralized nature comes with significant risks, including vulnerability to cyberattacks and reliance on trust in platform operators. Additionally, many CEXs require **KYC (Know Your Customer)** procedures, which can limit access for users seeking anonymity or residing in countries with regulatory restrictions.

12.2. Decentralized Exchange (DEX)

DEXs, or decentralized exchanges, operate without a centralized entity, using **smart contracts** to facilitate the direct exchange of assets between users. Among the most popular DEXs are **Uniswap**, the undisputed leader in the DeFi landscape on Ethereum, **SushiSwap**, which offers advanced features such as farming and staking, and **PancakeSwap**, dominant in the Binance Smart Chain. Other notable names include **Curve**, which specializes in stablecoin exchanges, and **Balancer**, which allows you to create custom liquidity pools.

In DEXs, users retain full control over their funds, which remain in their wallets until a trade is made. Most DEXs use **Automated Market Maker (AMM)** models, where asset prices are determined by liquidity pools and algorithms, rather than a traditional order book.

DEXs offer significant benefits, such as increased security due to the absence of centralized custody and unrestricted access. You don't need to ledger or provide any personal data, giving you more privacy than CEXs. However, they have some limitations, including lower liquidity than CEXs, high costs due to network fees (especially on Ethereum), and increased technical complexity, which can be a barrier for new users.

13. Wallet

A **wallet** (digital wallet) is an essential tool for interacting with blockchains and managing cryptocurrencies and, for all intents and purposes, constitutes a functional component of the blockchain. Without the wallet, in fact, users could not create transactions so the entire blockchain would be useless.

Unlike a traditional physical wallet, a wallet does not store tokens directly but stores cryptographic keys that allow access to the funds recorded on the blockchain. These keys are the heart of the cryptocurrency security system and are divided into two main types: **public key** and **private key**.

A **private key** is a randomly generated secret code, usually consisting of a long string of alphanumeric characters. This key represents full access to the associated funds and allows transactions to be digitally signed, ensuring that they are authentic and authorized by the owner. The private key must be guarded with extreme care, as anyone who comes into possession of it can access and use the associated cryptocurrencies without any possibility of canceling or recovering any transfers.

To facilitate management and reduce the risk of errors in copying or transcribing the private key, many wallets offer the option of saving it in the form of a **sequence of words**, known as a **seed phrase** or recovery phrase. This sequence, usually consisting of 12, 18, or 24 common words, is generated following cryptographic standards (such as BIP-39) and represents a readable and more practical version of the private key. The seed phrase can be used to recreate the private key and therefore access the wallet, making it essential for recovering funds in the event of loss or damage to the device on which the wallet is installed.

Thanks to this system, the risk of manual errors, such as the wrong entry of the alphanumeric key, is significantly reduced. However, the seed phrase must be protected with the same care as the private key, as anyone who owns it can rebuild the wallet and access the funds. Using secure methods to store it, such as writing it down to a physical medium and storing it in a safe place, is crucial for ensuring the security of your wallet and cryptocurrency.

The **public key**, which is mathematically derived from the private key through asymmetric encryption algorithms (such as ECDSA, Elliptic Curve Digital Signature Algorithm), is used to receive funds. From the public key, the **address** is obtained, which is a shorter and more readable representation, obtained by applying a hashing algorithm (such as SHA-256 followed by RIPEMD-160, for example in the case of Bitcoin) to the public key. The address is what is shared with other people to receive cryptocurrencies and is unique to each wallet.

13.1. Types of Wallets

Wallets are mainly divided into **hot wallets** and **cold wallets**, depending on whether they are connected to the internet or not. A **hot wallet**, such as MetaMask, Trust Wallet, or Coinbase Wallet, is always online and allows for quick and convenient access to funds. However, the constant connection to the internet makes them more vulnerable to cyberattacks.

A **cold wallet**, on the other hand, such as Ledger or Trezor, is a physical device or offline solution that is not connected to the internet. This makes them extremely secure for long-term storage of cryptocurrencies, as private keys are never exposed to potential online threats.

13.2. How a Wallet works

A wallet operates as an interface to interact with the blockchain. When a user wants to send cryptocurrencies from their own addresses, the wallet creates the body of the transaction following the standard protocol and uses the private key to sign it. The body of the transaction includes the public key, which will allow anyone who receives it to verify its authenticity. The signed transaction is then transmitted to the blockchain network, where nodes verify and record the transaction.

To receive funds, the wallet monitors the blockchain for transactions associated with its address.

The concept can then be extended to any type of digital object managed by a blockchain, which is structured according to a standard supported by the wallet. For example, in addition to an income statement, a wallet can display a collection of NFTs, non-fungible tokens linked to media stored off-chain, or a list of Decentralized Identities (DIDs) and a list of Verifiable

Credentials. Each of these objects has specific properties and methods that can be viewed and activated through the wallet.

13.3. Wallet Custodial and Non-Custodial

There are two main approaches to managing wallets: **custodial** and **non-custodial**. In custodial wallets, such as those offered by centralized exchanges, it is the service that stores the private keys on behalf of the user. This simplifies the user experience but sacrifices direct control over funds. These are in fact centralized services that could suddenly become inaccessible, making it impossible to withdraw your funds.

In non-custodial wallets, on the other hand, the user holds the private keys, guaranteeing full autonomy and sovereignty over their cryptocurrencies. However, this comes with a greater responsibility: the loss of the private key is equivalent to the irreversible loss of funds.

13.4. Security and Importance of the Wallet

The wallet is a crucial element for the security of cryptocurrencies. Protecting private keys is critical, and best practices include the use of strong passwords, secure backups, and, when possible, the adoption of hardware wallets to store funds offline. Thanks to advanced cryptography and mathematical key generation, wallets guarantee a high level of security. However, the ultimate responsibility always remains with the user, who must manage their digital assets with care and awareness.

14. Blockchain-based applications

A long time ago, computer applications were isolated programs that provided specific functionality on their own. Over time, the need to collaborate and share data led to the emergence of **client-server** architecture, where a server application supports multiple client applications, allowing them to interact and exchange information. Later, with the advent of the web, this architecture evolved into the **client-front-end-back-end** model. In this configuration, the back-end plays the role of the central server, while the front-end, usually a web server, supports web-apps, i.e. applications that publish data and interact with the client using the HTML standard. The client, often a browser, interprets HTML and its protocols to provide a user interface.

This model has simplified application development, as the client does not have to be designed for each specific application; A standard browser ensures compatibility and security. The development of the front-end has also been facilitated by the use of thousands of pre-configured templates, applicable to different contexts, such as e-commerce sites, games or monitoring systems. In addition, the back-end has been simplified thanks to the integration of advanced databases, which offer features dedicated to data management and processing.

With the advent of **cloud computing**, this architectural model has undergone further evolution. Server and application virtualization has introduced efficient and flexible building blocks, reducing management complexity for developers and businesses. However, the security of the entire system has remained the responsibility of those who develop the applications and manage the architecture. The growing threat of cyberattacks has made this aspect increasingly critical and complex to manage.

14.1. Blockchain as an architectural evolution

To address these challenges, a new architectural evolution is emerging: the **client-blockchain** model, which takes up the client-server concept but moves much of the server's functionality to the blockchain, implementing them through **smart contracts**. In this setup, operational security is ensured by the blockchain infrastructure itself, which is why it is crucial to use blockchains with a high level of security.

The client in this architecture is called a **dApp** (distributed application) and includes the wallet to protect users' private keys. This approach reverses the traditional paradigm: while in the client-server model the back end is protected, in a dApp it is the front-end that requires more attention to ensure security and privacy. Despite this, it is important to note that blockchain is not a direct alternative to a database. Not all client-server applications can be automatically transferred to a blockchain, as this technology is designed to produce consensus on certain types of data.

In fact, blockchain produces consensus exclusively on deterministic processes in which each future state is entirely predictable starting from the current state without the intervention of randomness and **Markovian stochastic** processes, where the future state of a system depends solely on the current state, without direct influences from previous states.

A typical example is the balance of an income statement, which can be calculated from the current balance and future transactions. This model allows complex behaviors to be represented and managed in a probabilistic way, making blockchain ideal for automating logical processes that require randomness or dynamic variations.

However, not all processes fit this logic. Data from **non-Markovian or non-deterministic** processes, such as temperature detected by an environmental sensor, cannot be verified by the blockchain. In these cases, the blockchain can only store them, making the operation often inefficient due to the high storage costs. For this reason, it is necessary to carefully evaluate the use of blockchain as a simple storage system, adopting it only when there are specific needs or solutions to manage data that are no longer needed.

Practical example of using blockchain to make an industrial application more robust: in the context of logistics applications, blockchain offers powerful tools to represent real processes. A non-fungible token can be used to represent a package, with unique properties such as identifier, weight, and size. The movement of this package from one warehouse to another can be represented as a transaction on the blockchain, where the package is transferred from one address to another. The blockchain ensures the uniqueness of the package and prevents duplication or unauthorized transfers.

If you use the **Move VM,** you can develop even more advanced smart contracts that model process-specific objects, such as "package" or "warehouse." These objects can have defined properties, such as identifier or address, and associated methods, such as "transfer." A transaction can then invoke the "transfer" method to move package "XYZ" from warehouse "A" to warehouse "B".

The blockchain's ability to handle both economic and logical transactions expands its possibilities of use. This technology, if designed correctly, can become a versatile platform for a wide range of business applications, from logistics to finance, digital identity management and supply chain. However, its use requires a deep understanding of its limitations, costs and opportunities, to ensure that the added value outweighs the complexities introduced.

14.2. How to design dApps

Designing blockchain-based applications involves a number of fundamental considerations that differ significantly from traditional architectures. When **smart contracts** represent a key component of architecture, important implications emerge related to their public nature and how they interact with them.

One of the main aspects to consider is that a smart contract published on a blockchain is accessible by anyone, as well as the data it produces or receives. This can be a problem if the contract is not designed to adequately handle external requests or to restrict access to certain features. However, it can turn into a strategic advantage if the contract includes a mechanism that requires the payment of a **fee for each execution**, regardless of who activates it. This model allows you to directly monetize the use of the contract, making it cost-effective even for public use scenarios.

Designing blockchain-based applications requires an **architectural paradigm shift**. In a typical traditional application, the heart of the process resides in the server or back-end, infrastructure components that are normally protected from unauthorized access and centrally controlled. In a blockchain-based application, on the other hand, the inherent security of the network and smart contracts allows the main logic to be moved directly to the smart contract, which becomes publicly accessible.

As a result, the focus on security shifts to the **client**, i.e. the dApp, typically a web app or mobile app where it incorporates the **user's wallet**. Protecting the private keys within the wallet becomes critical, as these keys are the only means of authorizing transactions or interacting with the smart contract. In this context, it is essential to implement advanced security mechanisms in the dApp, such as multi-factor authentication, encryption of local keys, and the use of hardware wallets.

Alternatively, it is possible to separate the application logic from the economic management implemented by the wallet, creating a "gas station", i.e. a server that receives application transactions from dApps and adds the economic component (fees necessary to pay for the smart contract).

Another crucial aspect in the design of blockchain applications concerns the data published on the network. The blockchain, by its nature, is a public ledger, which implies that any recorded data becomes accessible to everyone. This raises significant challenges in terms **of data privacy** and GDPR (General Data Protection Regulation) compliance.

To comply with regulation and ensure user privacy, it is critical to design your application so that:

- **Sensitive data is not directly stored on the blockchain.** Instead, you can use techniques such as **tokenization** or **off-chain storage**, where only cryptographic references or hashes are recorded on the blockchain.
- **Smart contracts are designed to minimize the exposure of personal information.** This can include the use of anonymization algorithms or zero-knowledge proof, which allow certain conditions to be verified without revealing underlying data.
- **Users have full control over their data.** Applications must implement mechanisms to allow users to manage and revoke access to their data, in line with the principles of the GDPR.

14.3. Decentralized Finance (DeFi): Revolution in Financial Services

DeFi represents one of the most transformative applications of blockchain in the financial sector. Based on smart contracts, DeFi eliminates the need for traditional intermediaries such as banks and brokers, offering direct financial services between users. DeFi platforms allow for lending, asset swapping, staking, yield farming, and much more, using automated and transparent protocols.

A significant example is **Uniswap**, a decentralized exchange (DEX) that uses an Automated Market Maker (AMM) model to allow token swaps without the need for a traditional order book. Another case is **Aave**, a platform that allows users to lend and borrow cryptocurrencies, earn interest or paying competitive fees. DeFi is revolutionizing traditional banking, making financial services accessible to anyone in the world, as long as they have an internet connection.

14.4. NFT

Non-Fungible Tokens (NFTs) are unique tokens that can be used to represent digital ownership of objects or content, such as art, music, videos, or even virtual land. Their uniqueness is guaranteed by smart contracts that make each NFT verifiable and unrepeatable.

In business, NFTs are opening up new opportunities for artists, content creators, and businesses. Platforms such as **OpenSea** and **Rarible** allow artists to sell digital works directly to collectors, eliminating intermediaries and guaranteeing automatic royalties on subsequent sales. In addition to the art world, NFTs also find application in the gaming industry, where they are used to represent virtual goods such as weapons, skins, or characters, often tradable in secondary markets.

14.5. Traceability: Transparency in the supply chain

One of the areas where blockchain has found a practical and highly effective application is traceability in the supply chain. The blockchain's ability to record data in an immutable and transparent way allows companies to monitor every stage of production and distribution, ensuring authenticity and quality.

For example, companies in the agri-food sector use blockchain to trace the path of products, from cultivation to the end consumer. Projects such as those of **IBM Food Trust** (which, however, is not a private blockchain, i.e. with "permissioned" nodes) offer solutions to trace the origin and transport conditions of food, increasing consumer trust and reducing the risks of fraud or contamination.

The luxury sector is also leveraging blockchain to combat counterfeiting. Brands such as **Louis Vuitton** and **Cartier** use blockchain-based platforms to provide digital certificates that attest to the authenticity of their products, ensuring that customers are buying original goods.

14.6. Notarization: immutability and validity of documents

Digital **notarization** is another blockchain-based service that is gaining popularity in the business world. With blockchain's ability to record data immutably, it is possible to create digital ledgers that serve as proof of the existence, ownership, or integrity of documents.

For example, platforms such as **Propy** allow real estate properties to be registered on the blockchain, ensuring the validity of documents and reducing costs related to traditional bureaucracy. Other applications include filing contracts, patents, legal or academic documents, providing verifiable proof of their authenticity and date of creation.

Blockchain notarization is particularly useful in industries where security and transparency are crucial, such as digital identity management or intellectual property protection.

15. Decentralized identity

A special and extremely important case of application, optionally based on blockchain, is decentralized **identity (DID).** This paradigm aims to overcome the limitations of traditional centralized systems, which rely on intermediary authorities to verify and manage individuals' personal information. Using **DIDs** and blockchain technologies, decentralized identity offers a unique combination of individual control, privacy, and security.

15.1. DID e DID Document

At the heart of decentralized identity is DID, a globally unique identifier that can be associated with a person, organization, or even a device (even passive, i.e., non-digital). Unlike traditional identifiers, such as document numbers or email addresses, a DID is not issued or controlled by a central authority but is user-generated and registered in a decentralized network.

Each DID is associated with a **DID Document**, a structured file that contains information critical to verifying the DID. This information includes:

- The public keys associated with the DID, which are used to authenticate the identifier check.
- Metadata that describes the available verifiable communication methods or credentials.
- Any endpoints to interact with the subject represented by the DID.

The **DID Document** can be stored in a blockchain, making it accessible to anyone who needs it. This choice guarantees transparency and immutability: once registered, the document cannot be altered without the change being visible and verifiable by the entire network.

15.2. A practical use case for DID

Let's imagine a user who wants to access a website to book a service. Using their digital wallet (DID wallet), the user can authenticate without having to create a traditional account: when the user logs in, the site sends a request to the wallet to obtain the DID and be able to retrieve the DID Document from the specific container indicated in its own code. The DID Document contains the user's public key that can be used to verify the digital signature generated by the wallet during authentication. If the verification is successful, the site can be sure that the user is the one who checks the DID.

In turn, the user can request the site to present its own DID and activate the authentication procedure. This **mutual identification** process ensures that the user is not interacting with a fraudulent site. For example, the site's DID Document might contain a verifiable credential issued by a recognized certificate authority, confirming its legitimacy.

Once this phase is over, both can deepen the level of identification by exchanging verifiable credentials.

15.3. Verifiable Credentials

Verifiable credentials (VCs) are another key element of decentralized identity. A VC is a digital certificate issued by a trusted authority, such as a government or bank, and digitally signed. It may attest to specific information about the user, such as the age of majority, residence or educational qualification.

In our example, you could use a VC to prove that you are of legal age without revealing any additional personal details, such as your full date of birth. The site verifies the credential by consulting the blockchain to confirm the authenticity of the digital signature of the issuing authority. Similarly, the website could produce a VC, issued for example by the chamber of commerce, which certifies its authenticity, effectively eliminating any risk of phishing.

The combination of DID, DID Document, and VC makes the system extremely secure and resilient, ensuring that only authentic and authorized information is shared.

15.4. Benefits of Decentralized Identity

The use of the blockchain-registered DID Document eliminates the need for centralized intermediaries to verify identities. This approach not only improves security, but also provides more transparency. Users retain full control over their data and only share the information that is strictly necessary for each interaction. The ability to verify the DID Document in a public and secure way reduces the risk of fraud and phishing, creating a more reliable digital ecosystem.

For the service provider, decentralized identity simplifies access management and reduces the costs associated with protecting personal data. In addition, the mutual identification process improves trust between users and services, encouraging safer and more efficient interactions.

16. Conclusions

Blockchain is one of the most promising technologies of our time, capable of radically transforming the way data, transactions and digital interactions are managed. Far from being a simple distributed ledger, blockchain is a complex and versatile ecosystem, built on mathematical principles and consensus protocols that ensure security, decentralization and immutability.

Soon, blockchain will continue to evolve, addressing crucial challenges such as balancing scalability, security, and decentralization. The **blockchain trilemma**, which represents the difficulty of excelling in these three dimensions at the same time, will stimulate the development of new technical solutions. Models such as **sharding, layer 2,** and the use of directed acyclic graphs (**DAGs**) already demonstrate the potential to overcome current limitations, paving the way for greater efficiency and adoption.

The integration of blockchain with other emerging technologies, such as artificial intelligence and the Internet of Things, will bring new opportunities. The tokenization of assets, the creation of decentralized finance (DeFi) ecosystems, the implementation of secure digital identities, and traceability in the supply chain are just some of the fields in which blockchain could redefine standards, improving transparency, trust, and accessibility.

However, large-scale adoption will require more than just technological innovations. An open and constructive dialogue between developers, regulators, companies and users will be essential. Regulations, such as those proposed by the European Union with the introduction of **MiCA** (Markets in Crypto-Assets), represent an important step in creating a clear and shared framework, promoting trust without stifling innovation.

Blockchain has the potential to become the foundation of a safer, more inclusive and sustainable digital world. Its applications will continue to expand, not only in the management of economic transactions, but also in the creation of completely new ecosystems based on automation and decentralization. The future of blockchain will depend on the collective ability to seize its opportunities and address its complexities, turning it into a force that redefines the foundations of our digital society.

www.ingramcontent.com/pod-product-compliance
Lightning Source LLC
La Vergne TN
LVHW052305060326
832902LV00021B/3719